Botanical
Metamorphosis
**Hideyuki
Niwa**

Botanical
Metamorphosis
Hideyuki
Niwa

Botanical Metamorphosis
Hideyuki Niwa

stichting kunstboek

Preface

By developing a special sense or awareness for flowers and plants, by always being on the lookout for them, and by trying to see flowers and plants from a new point of view, you will see 'something'.

The expression in flower heads, the movement – the 'breathing' – of leaves, the heart beating in the stems and the will of branches... Capture every moment in the blink of an eye.

In order to enhance the charm of nature captured, one must 'dismantle' the original shapes, 'reconstruct' them and awaken a new kind of beauty.

This is Botanical Metamorphosis.

———

感覚を研ぎ澄まし、
常に新しい視点で、花・植物と向き合うことにより、
みえてくるものがある。

花の表情、葉の息遣い、茎の鼓動、枝の意思…。
逃さないように、瞬時に捉える。

捉えた魅力を最大限に引き出すため、
本来の姿から「解体・再構築」を繰り返し、
新たな美を覚醒させる。

これがBotanical Metamorphosisである。

6 — 7

Sharpness — 鋭さ

10 — 11

Shade — 陰影

Equilibrium — 均衡

Quietness — 静寂なる

leave us alone #001 — ここにいたい #001

Feeling of Sakura #001 — 桜の気持ち #001

Feeling of Sakura #002 — 桜の気持ち #002

Even If It Falls — 散ってても

Till the End — 最後まで

Tense Atmosphere #001 — 張り詰めた空気 #001

Tense Atmosphere #002 — 張り詰めた空気 #002

Meant to be #001 — なるべくして #001

Shape of Vase #001 — 器の形 #001

Naked ― 一糸まとわぬ

Let Me Hear Your Voice ― 聴かせて

Sun Trail — 陽の記憶

Moon Trail ― 月の記憶

Gloomy Poppy ― 憂鬱なポピー

Fluttering in the Dark — 闇夜に舞う

Circle of life ― 始まりがあれば

Dwelling — すみか

Shyness — 恥じらい

Piece of Memory — 記憶の断片

Fog — 霧

Vague Contour — やわらかな輪郭

Jump for Joy — 溢れる想い

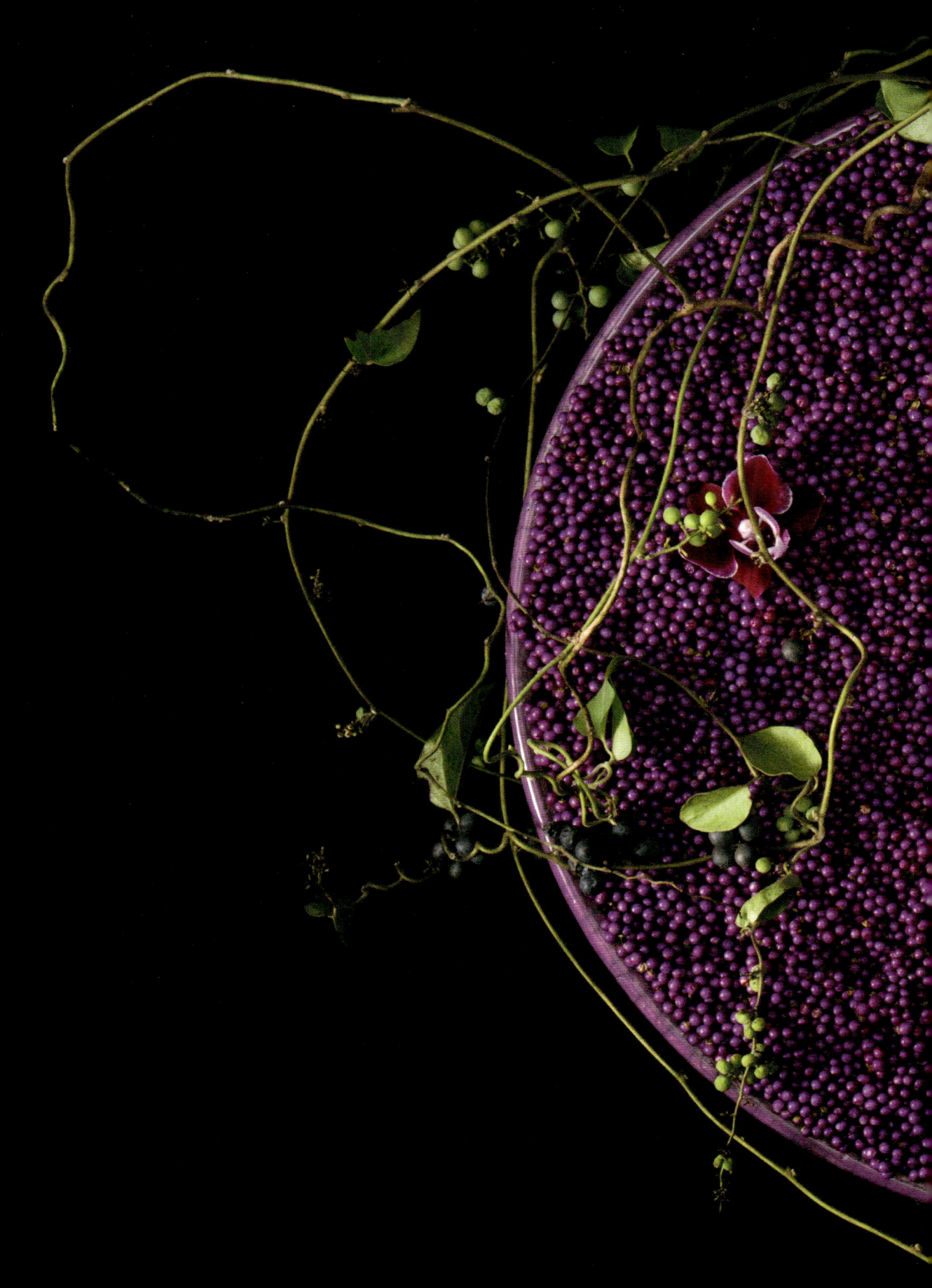

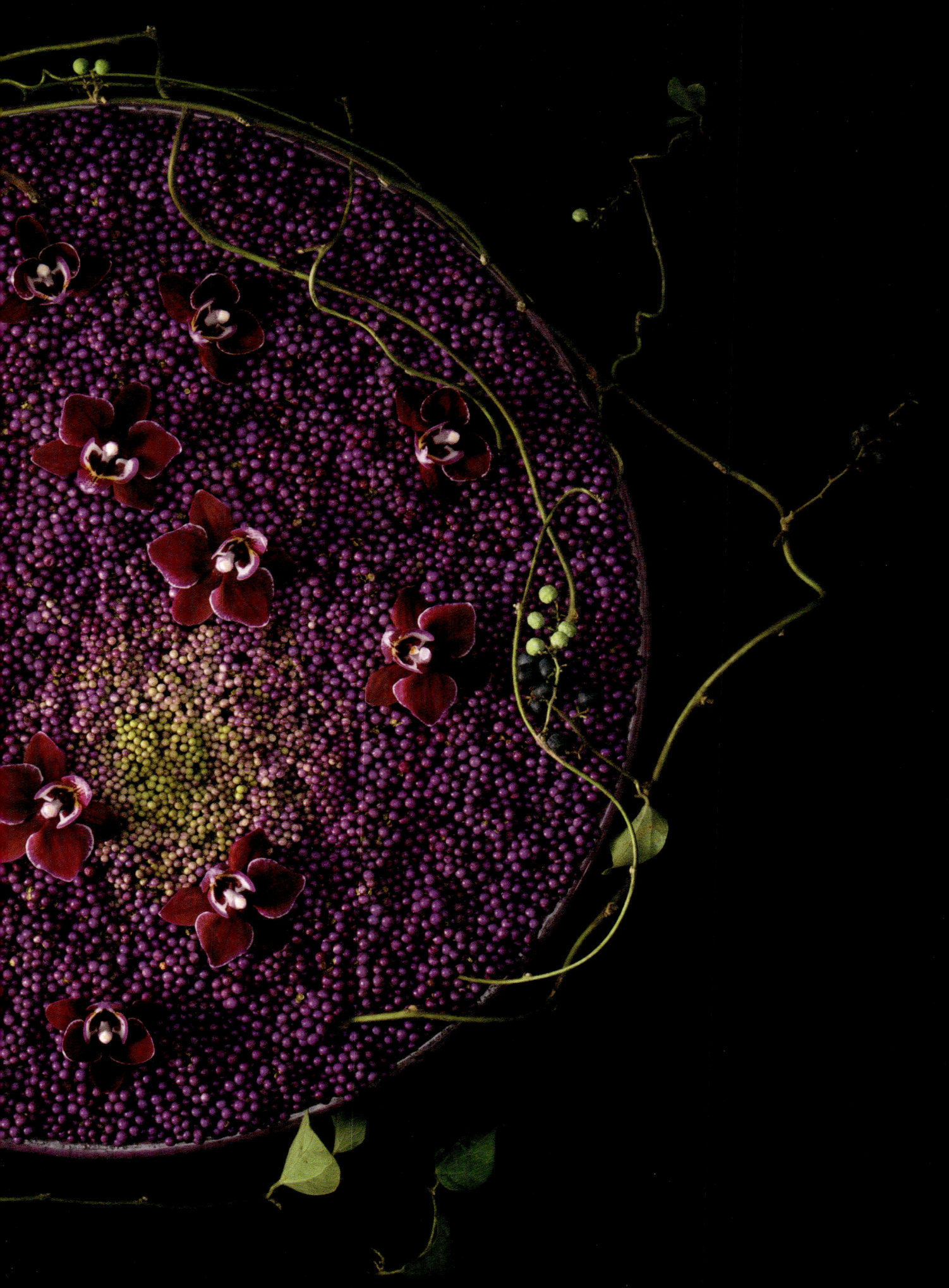

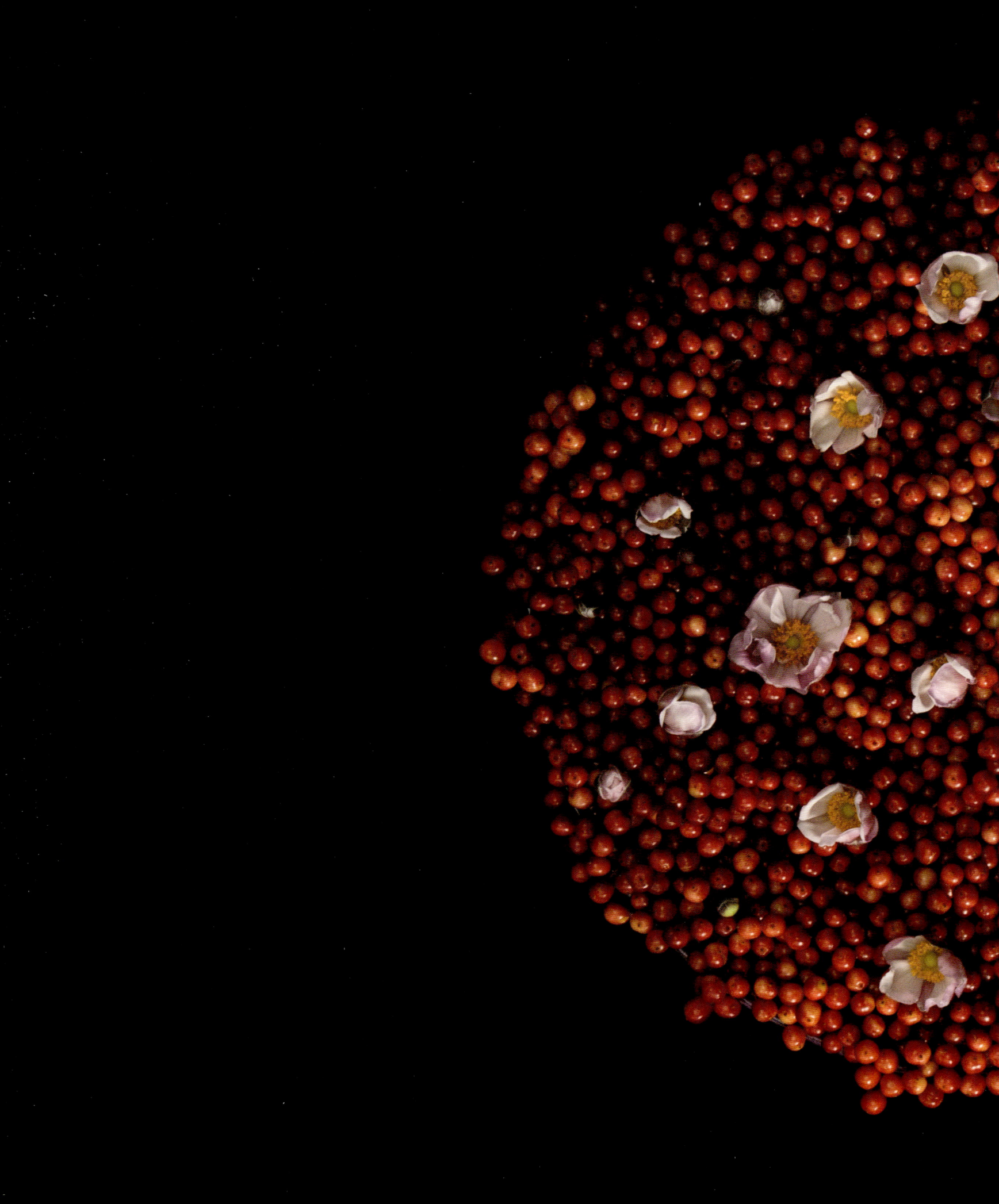

Maturity — 成熟

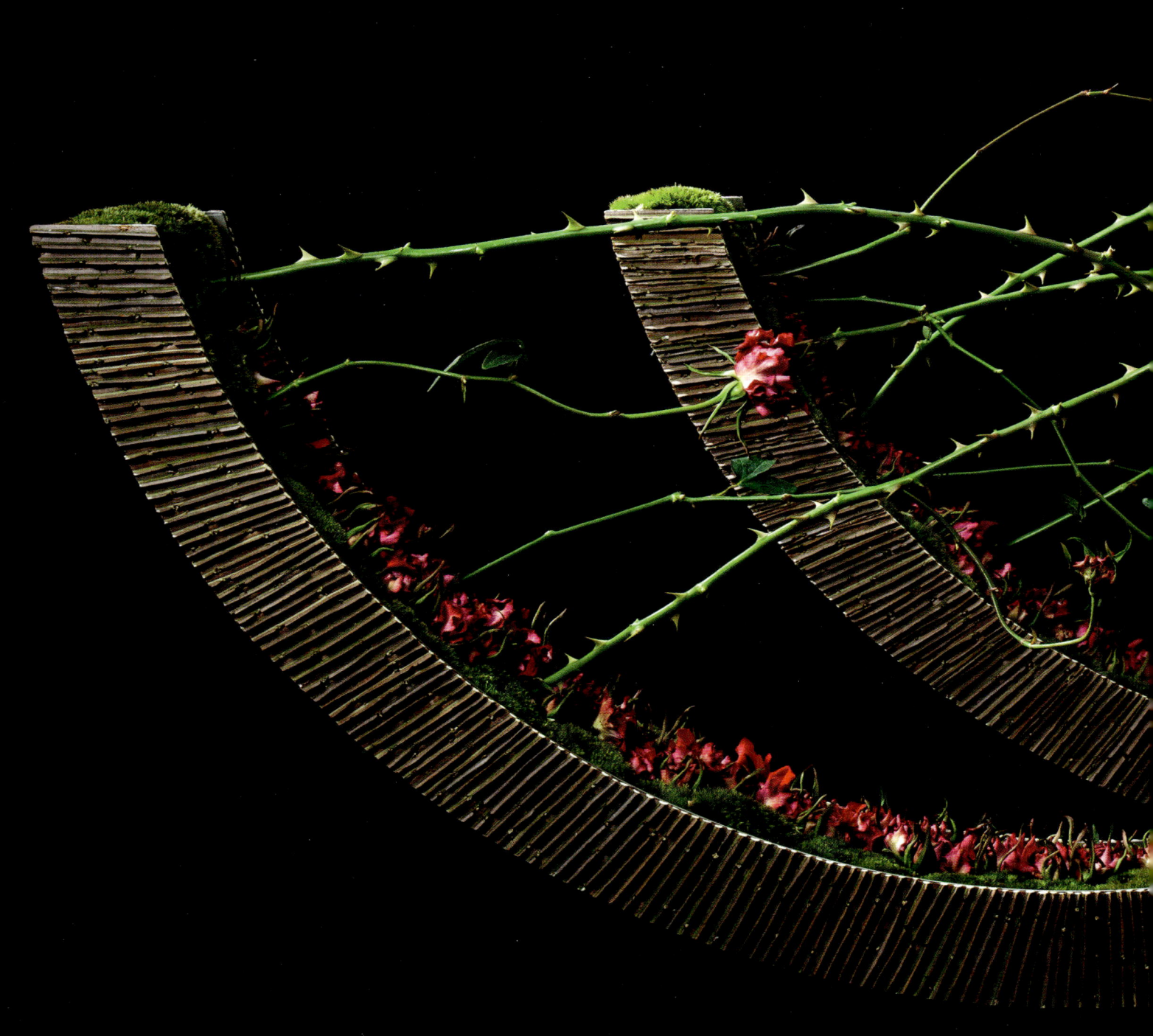

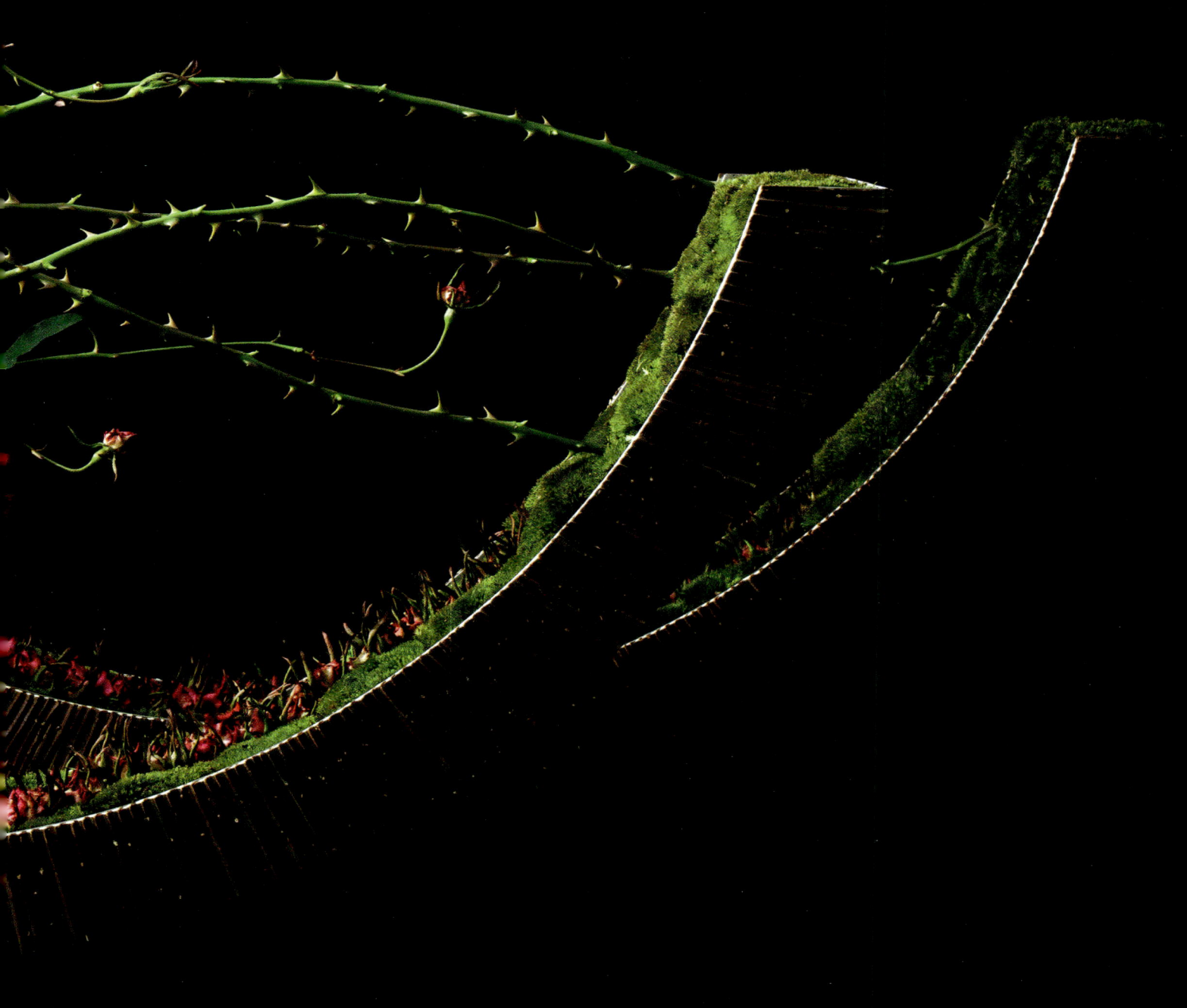

Beating — 鼓動

Everlasting Time ─ 永遠なる時間

Eternal Roses — 永遠なる薔薇

Eternal Roses ― 永遠なる薔薇

Inward #005 Silence — うちなるもの #005 響音

#004 Impulse ― うちなるもの #004 衝動

Finding Light — 光源を探す

Spiritual Boundary — 結界

Title / flowers

Cover
Beating —— 鼓動
Xanthorrhoea | Rosa

p.2
Equilibrium —— 均衡
Xanthorrhoea | Rosa

p.5
Fog —— 霧
Pinus

p.6 – 7
Sharpness —— 鋭さ
Xanthorrhoea | Clematis

p.8 – 9
Love-Hate —— 愛憎
Rosa

p.10 – 11
Shade —— 陰影
Xanthorrhoea

p.12 – 13
Equilibrium —— 均衡
Xanthorrhoea | Rosa

p.14 – 15
Quietness —— 静寂なる
Tulipa

p.16
Leave us alone #001 —— ここにいたい #001
Tulipa

p.17
Leave us alone #002 —— ここにいたい #002
Tulipa

p.18
Feeling of Sakura #001 —— 桜の気持ち #001
Prunus lannesiana

p.19
Feeling of Sakura #002 —— 桜の気持ち #002
Prunus lannesiana

p.20 – 21
Even If It Falls —— 散ってこそ
Prunus pendula Maxim

p.22 – 23
Till the End —— 最後まで
Prunus pendula Maxim

p.24 – 25
Tense Atmosphere #001 —— 張り詰めた空気 #001
Freesia

p.26 – 27
Tense Atmosphere #002 —— 張り詰めた空気 #002
Freesia

p.28
Meant to be #001 —— なるべくして #001
Magnolia kobus

p.29
Meant to be #002 —— なるべくして #002
Viola

p.30
Shape of Vase #001 —— 器の形 #001
Cornus florida

p.31
Shape of Vase #002 —— 器の形 #002
Chrysanthemum | Viburnum furcatum

p.32 – 33
Voice —— 声
Helleborus | Spiraea cantoniensis | Pisum sativum

p.34 – 35
Naked —— 一糸まとわぬ
Tulipa

p.36 – 37
Breath —— 吐息
Convallaria majalis

p.38 – 39
Let Me Hear Your Voice —— 聴かせて
Muscari

p.40
Sun Trail —— 陽の記憶
Dahlia | Euonymus alatus

p.41
Moon Trail —— 月の記憶
Dahlia | Euonymus alatus

p.42 – 43
Gloomy Poppy —— 憂鬱なポピー
Papaver rhoeas

p.44 – 45
Fluttering in the Dark —— 闇夜に舞う
Rosa | Leucobryum neilgherrense

p.46
Circle of Life —— 始まりがあれば
Rosa

p.48
Dwelling —— すみか
Miscanthus sinensis | Clematis

p.49
Fit —— はまる
Asplenium nidus | Curcuma

p.50
Shyness —— 恥じらい
Muscari

p.51
Piece of Memory —— 記憶の断片
Gypsophila | Chamaecyparis pisifera var.squarrosa

p.52 – 53
Fog —— 霧
Pinus

p.54 – 55
Vague Contour —— やわらかな輪郭
Cotinus coggygria | Clematis

p.56 – 57
Secret —— 内緒
Oxypetalum | Magnolia grandiflora | Skimmia

p.58 – 59
Jump for Joy —— 溢れる想い
Callicarpa japonica | Clematis

p.60 – 61
Infinity —— 無限
Callicarpa japonica | Cocculus orbiculatus | Phalaenopsis

p.62 – 63
Maturity —— 成熟
Viburnum opulus 'Compactum' | Anemone hupehensis var. japonica

p.64 – 65
Pulsation —— 脈動
Rosa | Euonymus alatus | Leucobryum neilgherrense

p.66 – 67
Beating —— 鼓動
Xanthorrhoea | Rosa

p.68 – 69
Everlasting Time —— 永遠なる時間
Quercus myrsinifolia | Wax

p.70 – 71
Eternal Roses —— 永遠なる薔薇
Rosa

p.72 – 73
Eternal Roses —— 永遠なる薔薇
Rosa

p.74 – 75
Harmonious #002 —— 調和 #002
Euonymus alatus | Enkianthus perulatus | Chrysanthemum | Leucobryum neilgherrense

p.76 – 77
One by One —— たがえる
Schoenus melanostachys | Rosa | Dahlia | Clematis | Hydrangea | Elaeagnus

p.78 – 79
Afterglow —— 余韻
Schoenus melanostachys

p.80 – 81
Inward #005 Silence —— うちなるもの #005 響静
Schoenus melanostachys | Rosa

p.82
Inward #005-01 Hidden —— うちなるもの #005-01 秘めたる
Schoenus melanostachys | Rosa

p.83
Inward #004-01 Hidden —— うちなるもの #004-01 秘めたる
Cissus sicyoides | Rosa

p.84 – 85
Inward #004 Impulse —— うちなるもの #004 衝動
Cissus sicyoides | Rosa

p.86
Finding Light —— 光源を探す
Xanthorrhoea

p.87
Waterfall —— 水簾
Xanthorrhoea

p.88
Spiritual Boundary —— 結界
Bambuseae

p.89
Aurora —— 紅気
Cornus alba 'Sibirica' | Rosa multiflora

p.90 – 91
Vigor —— 余勢
Magnolia quinquepeta | Paeonia lactiflora

Through the expression of flowers, I am seeking 'something' that touches people's hearts.
I keep exploring an expression that goes beyond the beauty, tenderness and power that flowers and plants originally possess. Eccentric ideas or flashy accessories are unimportant. The most important thing is to feel the natural beauty of flowers and plants, and to enhance it.

It is my desire to bring out the secret beauty of nature, which no one notices, to cultivate it and to embody it in the world I want to express. I live my life and try to put all my feelings into flowers. An aspiration I am ready to pursue for the rest of my life. It has been 20 years since I started living with flowers, and I feel that I have finally arrived at the stage where I need to be to do this.

I do not expect that my works tug at the heartstring of all people, nor do I want to 'heal' them. But I believe that I can connect many people thanks to the attraction of my works. Usually, human relationships are not built in a day. However, encountering one strong or emotive design has great power. As soon as you rest your eyes on that special design, you will be inspired and enchanted. This extraordinary feeling cannot be described or expressed in words. These defining moments are rare in people's lives, so we need to cherish them.

I am wondering if my work could have that power. Even if I do not have an actual, physical connection with others, I am privileged to be able to connect and leave my mark on people thanks to my work as an artist. This is an important mission for any artist. I would be more than happy if my works find their way to somebody's heart, make a lasting impression, are fondly remembered and become something he or she would never forget. I will keep living and designing with flowers in the hope that this wish will come true.

Hideyuki Niwa

私は、花の表現を通じて、人の心を動かす「何か」を求めている。
そのために、花・植物が本来持つ美しさや優しさ、力強さを、一歩超える表現を探し続けている。
必要なことは、奇抜なアイディアや派手な仕掛けではない。一番大切なこと、それは、
花・植物の本来の美しさを感じとり、そして昇華させること。ここに至るか至らないかが、
大きな分かれ道だ。誰も気がつかないような植物の秘めた美しさを引き出し、表現したい世界を
具現化するための技術を磨き、そのために自身の全ての感覚を花に傾けて生きているか、
一生をかけて追究する覚悟があるかということだ。
花と向き合い20年が過ぎ、私は、ようやくこの門口に立てた。

私は、自身の作品が万人に癒やしを与えられるような、身近な存在になれるとは考えていないが、
作品を通じて、より多くの人と繋がることができると信じている。本来、人との繋がりとは、
すぐに生まれるものではなく、時間をかけてゆっくりと築いていくものだ。しかし、
一つの作品との出会いには、それを超越する力がある。出会った瞬間に、心動かされ、また、
心奪われる、言葉にはできないその感覚は、人生の中で何度も訪れることはない、特別な体験だ。

私の作品はそういった存在になれるだろうか。直接的な関わりや繋がりを持つことができなくとも、
作品を通じ、その人の人生に何か足跡を残せること、繋がりを持てること、
これは表現者に与えられた特権であり、また、使命でもある。ある瞬間から私の作品が心に残り、
ふと思い返され、そして忘れられない存在になってくれれば良い。
そう願い、これからも花と向き合い続ける。

丹羽 英之

Hideyuki Niwa

Hideyuki Niwa was born in 1973 in Aichi. His family runs a flower shop, so Hideyuki has spent his childhood surrounded by flowers. After graduating from college in Tokyo, he joined a leading flower shop in the same city, where he mastered the basic floristry skills. Having worked at a flower shop in Marunouchi, Tokyo as c chief designer and brand manager, he started his own design team 'Hideyuki Niwa Design Office'. He directed a lot of design works, such as floral decoration at various events and some large collaboration with brands. 'Imagining and Creating' is his concept. Hideyuki Niwa tries to pursue and create a new kind of beauty in nature by a process he calls 'botanical metamorphosis'. He holds exhibitions and workshops and has published a number of art books in Japan and abroad.

Personal History/Awards
2009 Produced floral design of wedding ceremony and room decoration,
    'AYANA Resort and Spa BALI', Indonesia
2012 Award Gold Leaf, 'International Floral Art 12/13', Belgium
    Solo Exhibition 'Hideyuki NIWA Contemporary Floral Art', Marunouchi, Tokyo
2013 First Place and a Prime Minister's Prize, JFTD Japan Cup 2013
    Solo Exhibition -eternal time-, Forum Art Shop Gallery in Tokyo International Forum
2014 Third Place, 'International Asian Cup 2014'
    Solo Exhibition -eternal time- 'Spring Forest', 'Winter Lake', Hiroshi Senju Museum Karuizawa Gallery
2016 Gold Award, 'Singapore Garden Festival 2016' under the 'Floral Art' category, Singapore
    Special Lecturer, Cohim Flower School Beijing. China
2017 General director, directed floral art and decoration,
    '2018 International Floral Design Trend Forum', Beijing, China

Publications
- Floral Art of JAPAN from now (Joint authorship・SODO Publishing/2010)
- Hideyuki Niwa Japanese Contemporary Floral Art (Stichting Kunstboek/2013)
- Great Flower Artists in Japan KAJIN (Joint authorship・SODO Publishing/2014)

———

丹羽 英之

1973年愛知県生まれ。生花店を営む家に生まれ、幼少の頃より花に親しむ。上京し、花の専門学校を卒業後、東京の大手生花店にてフローリストとしての基礎を学ぶ。東京丸の内のフラワーショップのチーフデザイナー・ブランドマネージャーを経て、デザインチームHideyuki Niwa Design Officeを立ち上げ、様々なイベントでの装花演出やブランドとのコラボレーションなどのデザインワークを行う。「想像し創造する」をコンセプトに掲げ、植物の解体再構築を繰り返す中で生まれる新たな美を追究し、国内外での作品展示やワークショップの開催、作品集出版など活動の幅を広げている。

主な経歴
2009 AYANA Resort & Spa BALIのウエディングフラワー及び館内装花をプロデュース
2012 ベルギー【International Floral Art 12/13】にて最優秀賞ゴールドリーフ賞受賞
    東京丸の内にて単独個展「Hideyuki NIWA Contemporary Floral Art」を開催
2013 一般社団法人日本生花通信配達協会主催 ジャパンカップ2013にて
    優勝・内閣総理大臣賞受賞
    フォーラム・アートショップ内ギャラリー(東京国際フォーラム)にて個展—eternal time-を開催
2014 フラワーデザイン国際競技会「アジアカップ2014」にて3位入賞
    軽井沢千住博美術館ギャラリーにて
    個展—eternal time-「Spring Forest」・「Winter Lake」を開催
2016 シンガポールガーデンフェスティバル2016フローラルアート部門にてゴールドアワード受賞
    中国北京 Cohim Flower School Beijing 特別講師に就任
2017 2018 International Floral Design Trend Forum (中国・北京)の総合演出
    会場フローラルアートを担当

著書
- 日本のフローラルアートのこれから (共著・草土出版/2010)
- Hideyuki Niwa Japanese Contemporary Floral Art (Stichting Kunstboek/2013)
- 時代を顕す 日本の花者(KAJIN) (共著・草土出版/2014)

Works / Text
Hideyuki Niwa — 丹羽 英之

Assistant
Chika Tsukada — 塚田 知佳

Photography
Kiyokazu Nakajima — 中島 清一
COHIM FLOWER SCHOOL p.86 – p.91

Translation
Sumire Harada — 原田 すみれ

Sponsor of photography
JR Nagoya Takashimaya — ジェイアール名古屋タカシマヤ
ALL TAKASHIMAYA AGENCY CO., LTD. — 株式会社 エー・ティ・エー
Art Print Japan Co., Ltd. — 株式会社 アートプリントジャパン
Museum of Contemporary Art Tokyo — 東京都現代美術館
COHIM FLOWER SCHOOL

Supported by
Hideyuki Niwa Design Office
Kamon Flower Gate Co., Ltd. — 株式会社 花門フラワーゲート
3-19-2 Hatchobori Chuo-ku Tokyo 104-0032, Japan — 〒104-0032 東京都中央区八丁堀3-19-2
Tel +81 3 5541 4187
Fax +81 3 5541 9887
http://hn-design.co.jp/
info@hn-design.co.jp

Final Editing
Katrien Van Moerbeke

Lay-out
Group Van Damme
www.groupvandamme.eu

Published by
Stichting Kunstboek bvba
Legeweg 165
BE-8020 Oostkamp
info@stichtingkunstboek.com
www.stichtingkunstboek.com

ISBN 978-90-5856-606-5
D/2018/6407/12
NUR 421

Printed in the EU

All rights reserved. No part of this book may be reproduced, stored in a datcbase or a retrieval system, or transmitted in any form or by any means, electronically, mechanically, by print, microfilm or otherwise without prior permission in writing from the publisher.

© Hideyuki Niwa, 2018
© Stichting Kunstboek bvba, 2018